VOCAL SELECTIONS

How To Succeed In Business Without Really Trying!

BOOK BY ABE BURROWS, JACK WEINSTOCK AND WILLIE GILBERT

BASED ON "HOW TO SUCCEED IN BUSINESS WITHOUT REALLY TRYING" BY SHEPHERD MEAD

MUSIC AND LYRICS BY FRANK LOESSER

The original Broadway production opened on October 14, 1961. The Broadway revival, pictured in this edition, opened on March 8, 1995.

Photos by Joan Marcus

Logo copyright © 1995 Doug Johnson

ISBN 0-88188-203-8

FRANK MUSIC CORP.

EXCLUSIVELY DISTRIBUTED BY

HAL•LEONARD® CORPORATION

7777 W. BLUEMOUND RD. P.O. BOX 13819 MILWAUKEE, WI 53213

Applications for performance of this work, whether legitimate,
stock, amateur or foreign, should be addressed to:
MUSIC THEATRE INTERNATIONAL
545 Eighth Avenue
New York, NY 10018

How To Succeed In Business Without Really Trying!

CONTENTS

BROTHERHOOD OF MAN

By FRANK LOESSER

LOVE FROM A HEART OF GOLD

By FRANK LOESSER

PARIS ORIGINAL

By FRANK LOESSER

HAPPY TO KEEP HIS DINNER WARM

By FRANK LOESSER

Happily, but not too fast

Lyrics:
I'll be so Hap - py To Keep His Din - ner Warm _____ while he goes on - ward _ and up - ward._

15

How to Succeed in Business Without Really Trying

Matthew Broderick, 1995 revival

The rapid rise of a personable young man from the bottom of the ranks of big business until he becomes Chairman of the Board is the theme of this Broadway Musical.

Our hero, J. Pierrepont Finch by name, pursues his goal of succeeding in business through a series of crafty, devious, impertinent and above all comic activities. He obtains his first position with the World Wide Wicket Co. and is assigned to the mail room, thus mounting on the first step on the ladder to success. However, the road to his ultimate goal is not without obstacles and pitfalls. Mr Biggley, the boss, has a nephew, Frump, working in the mailroom who also has ambitions to become head of the company. While Finch is likeable and smart, Frump is neither; but Frump is the boss's nephew. Needless to say, Frump is afraid of his competition and is constantly calculating ways of getting Finch in trouble.

Our hero also meets up with a beautiful secretary, Rosemary, who wants to become his wife, but J. Pierrepont Finch has little time for her because he is too busy rising from one position to another.

Soon Finch graduates from the mail room and obtains an office of his own, cramped and windowless, but all his own. He is assigned a gorgeous, siren-like secretary, Hedy, who cannot take shorthand or do any of the things a secretary is supposed to do. It is not long before Finch finds out that Hedy is the boss's girlfriend and uses her to his own advantage in upping his position. Shortly thereafter we find him in a huge office with windows and all the proper executive appointments.

Meanwhile all the girls at the office know that Rosemary loves Finch and they are all rooting for her to marry him. Finch on the other hand, is just too busy for love matters, his eye being on the job of the executive vice-president in charge of advertising.

Ronn Carroll and Matthew Broderick

In pursuit of advancement he has become a favorite of Mr Biggley, while alienating his fellow employees. He has come to Mr. Biggley's attention through a number of well-planned encounters. He intimates he went to the same college as Mr. Biggley (he did not); he implies he stays up night after night working on corporate matters (he does not); and that he has the same hobbies as Mr Biggley (he doesn't). However false these actions, they endear young Finch to the boss and when Finch points out that a new vice-president in charge of advertising went to a rival Alma Mater, Biggley fires him and appoints Finch to the job.

J. Pierrepont is now truly on the spot, for there has been a monthly succession of advertising vice-presidents, not one of them able to measure up to Biggley's standards. Finch is given 48 hours to make a presentation of a completely new advertising campaign.

Frump, sometime in the past, had presented an idea for a television quiz program which his uncle hated. Frump now seizes the opportunity to get rid of his rival, planting the old idea with Finch. Finch falls for the suggestion and bases his campaign around the old rejected idea. At the meeting of the executive committee, where Finch outlines his approach, he turns what appears to be a disaster into a triumph.

Mr Biggley buys Finch's elaboration of his nephew's old idea. The television show is presented to the public, but fails so badly there is little question that Finch is through for good.

At the end of the story our hero, appearing to be doomed, once again gains a stunning personal victory by some crafty maneuvering, is appointed Chairman of the Board, and of course marries Rosemary.

Matthew Broderick and Megan Mullally

I BELIEVE IN YOU

By FRANK LOESSER

HOW TO SUCCEED IN BUSINESS WITHOUT REALLY TRYING

By FRANK LOESSER

GRAND OLD IVY

By FRANK LOESSER

Interlude